CONTENTS

FOREST

THE 2019/20 SQUAD

Yuri RIBEIRO — 2

POSITION: Defender   **COUNTRY:** Portugal   **DOB:** 24 January 1997

Capped by Portugal at U21 level, left-back Yuri Ribeiro joined Nottingham Forest in July 2019 from Benfica. He arrived at the City Ground together with his former Benfica teammate Alfa Semedo. Ribeiro made his Forest debut in the League Cup first round victory over Fleetwood Town at the City Ground before then sampling the delight of an East Midlands derby victory over Derby County in the next round.

Costel PANTILIMON — 1

POSITION: Goalkeeper   **COUNTRY:** Romania   **DOB:** 1 February 1987

Romanian international goalkeeper Costel Pantilimon brings a wealth of experience to the Forest squad, following spells with Manchester City, Sunderland and Watford. The giant 'keeper initially joined Forest on loan in January 2018, before agreeing a permanent transfer in July 2018. After being first choice stopper throughout 2018/19, he now faces stiff competition for the No.1 position in Sabri Lamouchi's side.

Tobias FIGUEIREDO — 3

POSITION: Defender   **COUNTRY:** Portugal   **DOB:** 2 February 1994

An experienced defender, Tobias Figueiredo joined Forest on loan from Sporting Lisbon in January 2018 before then agreeing a permanent switch to the City Ground. Figueiredo has played in both Europa League and Champions League fixtures as well as representing his country at various youth levels. He featured in 13 Championship fixtures in the first half of the 2018/19 campaign and played in both of the club's League Cup victories in August 2019.

Joe
WORRALL

4

POSITION: Defender   **COUNTRY:** England   **DOB:** 10 January 1997

After spending the 2018/19 season on loan at Glasgow Rangers, central-defender Joe Worrall has returned to the City Ground determined to make a first-team place his own during the 2019/20 Championship campaign. The defender clearly made a positive impression on new boss Sabri Lamouchi who played Worrall in all eight of the club's fixtures in August 2019.

Alexander
MILOSEVIC

6

POSITION: Defender   **COUNTRY:** Sweden   **DOB:** 30 January 1992

Swedish international central-defender Alexander Milosevic joined Nottingham Forest on an 18-month deal in February 2019 after being brought to the club by former boss Martin O'Neill. A vastly-experienced defender, Milosevic featured in ten Championship fixtures following his arrival from Swedish side AIK and scored his first goal for the Reds in the 3-0 home win over Middlesbrough in April 2019.

THE LEGEND
PETER SHILTON

Goalkeeper Peter Shilton enjoyed a fantastic debut season with Nottingham Forest as the club were crowned First Division champions in 1977/78. Shilton conceded just 18 goals in 37 league appearances, with his most memorable performance coming in the title-clinching goalless draw with Coventry City. Shilton pulled off a remarkable save to prevent Mick Ferguson scoring for the Sky Blues with a powerful close-range header.

Shilton's outstanding performances in Forest's 1977/78 First Division title success saw the Reds' stopper voted the PFA Players' Player of the Year come the end of season. The award from his fellow professionals was a fitting reward for the consistency of his top quality performances in the Forest goal throughout a memorable campaign.

When First Division champions Nottingham Forest faced FA Cup winners Ipswich Town in the 1978 Charity Shield at Wembley in August, Peter Shilton enjoyed the satisfaction of a Wembley clean sheet as Forest got the new season off to a flying start with an emphatic 5-0 win at the Twin Towers.

Shilton played a vital role as Brian Clough's men became champions of Europe for the first time in 1979. Forest reached their first European Cup Final and faced Malmo in Munich on 30 May 1979. A Trevor Francis goal on the stroke of half time proved enough for Forest to win the match 1-0 as the ever-reliable Shilton kept a clean sheet at the other end.

As Nottingham Forest retained the European Cup in 1980, Peter Shilton once again produced a perfect performance in the final to record back-to-back European Cup Final clean sheets. On this occasion, Hamburg were the opposition and Madrid the venue, but there was still no getting the ball past Shilton.

JOE LOLLEY

2018/19

GOAL OF THE SEASON

Joe Lolley's long-range strike against Aston Villa was crowned Nottingham Forest's Goal of the Season for the 2018/19 campaign.

Following a fan vote, Lolley came out on top for his strike from 25 yards which flew into the top corner of the net to put the Reds in front at Villa Park in a thrilling match which ended 5-5.

Not only did Lolley score with a superb effort, he also provided all four of the assists for Forest's other goals, in a match which had everything, against the eventual Play-Off winners.

The first half ended 3-3 following a barnstorming start to the game, with Lewis Grabban slotting home from close range and Joao Carvalho latching on to Lolley's through ball to put Forest 2-0 up inside six minutes.

Tammy Abraham scored a three-minute brace to make it 2-2 before Matty Cash restored Forest's advantage on 22 minutes with a fine finish following Lolley's sliding through pass. Abraham's penalty on 36 minutes ensured he went home with the match ball and a thrilling first half ended all square.

Six minutes after half-time, Lolley hit his thunderous effort past goalkeeper Orjan Nyland, stunning the stopper and the packed crowd to restore the advantage for the Reds, then a red card for Tobias Figueiredo swung the game in Villa's favour.

Abraham's fourth of the game and a goal by Anwar El-Ghazi saw Villa go in front for the first time, but with eight minutes left on the clock, Lolley played in Grabban who finished neatly to secure a point on the most memorable of matches at Villa Park.

THE SHORTLIST

BEN OSBORN

Ben Osborn's superb turn and finish against Leeds United on New Year's Day came second in the Goal of the Season vote.

With Forest having just turned a 2-1 deficit into a 3-2 advantage, a counter attack down the left saw Daryl Murphy play in Osborn. He turned from his left foot to his right before unleashing an unstoppable shot into the net off the underside of the crossbar.

JOAO CARVALHO

A lovely one-two and finish from Joao Carvalho against Sheffield Wednesday saw his effort ranked third in the Goal of the Season vote.

The Portuguese creator curled a sumptuous effort into the top corner, out of the reach of keeper Cameron Dawson to seal a 2-1 victory at the City Ground.

Ben WATSON 8

POSITION: **Midfielder** COUNTRY: **England** DOB: **9 July 1985**

Famed for his winning FA Cup final goal for Wigan Athletic in 2013, experienced central-midfielder Ben Watson joined Forest in February 2018 from Watford. After 17 Championship appearances for the Reds in 2018/19, Watson was ever-present in Sabri Lamouchi's side across the opening month of league games in 2019/20 and looks set for a key role at the City Ground over the coming months.

Lewis GRABBAN 7

POSITION: **Striker** COUNTRY: **England** DOB: **12 January 1988**

Much-travelled Championship goal-getter Lewis Grabban joined Nottingham Forest in the summer of 2018 from Premier League Bournemouth. He ended his debut season at the City Ground as top scorer with 17 goals, 16 of which came in the league. Grabban hit the goal trail early in 2019/20 under the management of Sabri Lamouchi with four Championship goals in August 2019, including a brace in Forest's 2-1 win away to Fulham.

THE 2019/20 SQUAD

Joao CARVALHO — 10

POSITION: **Midfielder**   COUNTRY: **Portugal**   DOB: **9 March 1997**

Joao Carvalho scored the third and final goal of the game as Forest enjoyed a 3-0 League Cup second round victory over East Midlands rivals Derby County in August 2019. The match against the Rams was his first appearance under Sabri Lamouchi and the Portuguese midfielder certainly made the most of his opportunity to shine. Carvalho is now in his second season at the City Ground, having joined the club from Benfica in June 2018.

Matty CASH — 11

POSITION: **Midfielder**   COUNTRY: **England**   DOB: **7 August 1997**

A product of the Nottingham Forest Academy, midfielder Matty Cash appears all set for a starring role in the club's 2019/20 season. He began the new campaign by scoring the club's first goal of the season in the opening-day fixture against West Bromwich Albion. That goal against the Baggies came on the back of a 2018/19 campaign that saw Cash score eight goals, including two in the thrilling 3-3 draw with eventual champions Norwich City on Boxing Day 2018.

D Wears the Birmingham City captain's armband

Crystal Palace's nickname **E**

 Danish Head Coach at Griffin Park **F**

A Chelsea's Spanish skipper

The Toffees play their home games here **G**

B

Do you recognise this Championship club's crest

H Longest serving Championship manager and a Millwall legend

Scored the first home league goal of the season at the City Ground **C**

I Foxes' Nigeria international signing who wears No.8

A

FOREST

2019/20 — PART 1

WHO'S WHO & WHAT'S WHAT OF ENGLISH FOOTBALL?

J
Manchester City's Brazilian striker who was part of their 2019 Copa América winning side

L
This England international has been with the Red Devils since the age of 7

K
Polish international midfielder who was ever-present for Leeds United last season

M

The Seagulls' Premier League top scorer last season

15

ANSWERS ON PAGE 62

AT THE TRAINING GROUND

Come three o'clock on a Saturday afternoon, the fans get to see their heroes in action at the City Ground.

Matchday is the day Forest's players, manager and coaching staff are all preparing for, and focusing on, throughout the week. All that preparation takes place at the club's training ground, well away from the watching eyes of the thousands of fans who flock to the City Ground in hope of witnessing another winning performance.

The hard work begins in the summer months when the players report back for pre-season training. The players are given a fitness programme to follow over the summer break and the first few days back at the training ground tend to involve a number of fitness tests. The results will enable Sabri Lamouchi's coaching and fitness staff to assess each player's condition and level of fitness to ensure they are given the right workload over pre-season, so that they are fully match fit and raring to go for the big kick-off.

A lot of the work done over the pre-season period is designed to help the players reach a level of fitness that they can maintain for the entire campaign and perform at their maximum throughout the season.

When it comes to winning football matches, it is well known that practice, dedication and preparation are all vital ingredients for success. However, in terms of strength and fitness, rest, recovery and diet also play crucial roles in a footballer's welfare. The Forest players are not only given the best of surfaces to practice on, but also given expert advice and guidance to ensure that they are fully equipped for the Championship challenges ahead.

Technology also plays its part in helping the Forest stars perform to their maximum. Prior to taking to the training pitches, players are provided with a GPS tracking system and heart rate analysis monitors ensuring that all they do can be measured, monitored and reviewed.

And if all goes to plan, the team's drive, commitment and meticulous preparation on the training ground during the week, will pay dividends on matchday.

THE LEGEND
STUART PEARCE

Having arrived at the City Ground in 1985 following a transfer from Coventry City, Stuart Pearce soon made the Forest left-back berth his own. A star top-flight performer, Pearce's club form was swiftly rewarded with international recognition. His club and the Forest fans were delighted to see him make his England debut on 19 May 1987 as England drew 1-1 with Brazil at Wembley. It was the first of 78 caps he went on to win for his country.

As Forest captain, Pearce led the team out at Wembley behind manager Brian Clough for the 1988/89 League Cup Final meeting with Luton Town. Second-half goals from Nigel Clough (2) and Neil Webb saw Forest come from behind to win 3-1 and secure the League Cup for the third time in the club's history. A delighted Pearce then led his troops up the famous steps to collect the trophy.

Having got the taste for lifting silverware at Wembley, Pearce captained Forest to back-to-back League Cup triumphs. A year on from their 3-1 win over Luton Town, Pearce once again skippered his team to victory at Wembley in the League Cup Final. Oldham Athletic were the opposition as Nigel Jemson's 47th minute goal proved enough to sway the match in Forest's favour before Pearce once again hoisted the trophy.

The 1990/91 FA Cup Final saw Stuart Pearce score one of the most iconic goals in the club's history. The Wembley final was just 16 minutes old when Pearce smashed home one of his trademark thunderbolt free-kicks to put Forest in front. Sadly, Spurs recovered from falling behind and went on to win the match 2-1.

After Forest's disappointing relegation from the Premier League in 1992/93, Pearce remained loyal to the City Ground faithful and played a vital role in leading the club back to the top division at the first attempt. Under new manager Frank Clark, Pearce captained the side to the runners-up spot in the 1993/94 First Division table. Pearce featured in 42 of Forest's 46 league games in the 1993/93 promotion-winning season and also chipped in with six goals.

FAN TASTIC

There are five Great Sporting Brits hiding in the crowd...
Can you find them?

ANSWERS ON PAGE 62

THE 2019/20 SQUAD

Jordan SMITH

12

POSITION: **Goalkeeper** COUNTRY: **England** DOB: **8 December 1994**

A product of the Forest Academy, goalkeeper Jordan Smith has been with the club since the age of seven. He marked his full debut for the Reds with a clean sheet in a goalless draw against Wigan Athletic in February 2017. Smith has now made over 40 first-team appearances for Forest and taken in loan spells with Barnsley and Mansfield Town during the 2018/19 season.

John BOSTOCK

13

POSITION: **Midfielder** COUNTRY: **Trinidad & Tobago** DOB: **15 January 1992**

Former Crystal Palace and Tottenham Hotspur midfielder John Bostock, joined Forest in August 2019 on a season-long loan deal from French side Toulouse. A former England youth international, Bostock made his Forest debut in the League Cup match with Fleetwood before tasting Championship action when he appeared from the bench in the 1-1 draw away to newly-promoted Charlton Athletic.

Carl
JENKINSON
16

POSITION: **Defender**   COUNTRY: **England**   DOB: **8 February 1992**

A full England international, defender Carl Jenkinson brings a touch of Premier League class to the Forest backline following his August 2019 switch from Arsenal. Having played top-flight football for the Gunners, Jenkinson gained additional Premier League experience with a loan stint at West Ham United. His summer move to the City Ground was seen as a real coup for Forest and a true sign of the club's ambition.

Rafael
MIR
14

POSITION: **Striker**   COUNTRY: **Spain**   DOB: **18 June 1997**

Spanish U21 international frontman Rafael Mir joined Forest on loan from Premier League Wolverhampton Wanderers in the summer of 2019. With first-team chances few and far between at Molineux, Mir will certainly be looking to make his mark in the English game with Forest during the 2019/20 season. He made his debut on the opening day of the season, when he replaced Tiago Silva against West Bromwich Albion.

Alfa
SEMEDO
17

POSITION: **Midfielder**   COUNTRY: **Guinea-Bissau**   DOB: **30 August 1997**

Forest secured the signing of midfielder Alfa Semedo in a double swoop on Portuguese giants Benfica in the summer of 2019. After signing defender Yuri Ribeiro on a permanent basis, they also agreed a season-long loan deal for 22-year-old Semedo. Boss Sabri Lamouchi clearly has big plans for the player with him starting five of the club's first six Championship fixtures.

Can you figure out who these Forest stars are?

FACE

A

B

C

D

E

24

OFF!

1
2
3
4
5
6
7
8
9

ANSWERS ON PAGE 62

JOE WORRALL

**Colour in
this picture
of Forest star
Joe Worrall**

Sammy
AMEOBI

19

POSITION: **Midfielder**   COUNTRY: **England**   DOB: **1 May 1992**

Nottingham Forest agreed a one-year deal with powerful wideman Sammy Ameobi ahead of the 2019/20 season, after the player ended a two-year spell with Bolton Wanderers. He debuted in the opening-day clash with West Bromwich Albion at the City Ground and certainly made a positive impression on the Forest faithful during his first seven appearances for the club in August 2019.

Jack
ROBINSON

18

POSITION: **Defender**   COUNTRY: **England**   DOB: **1 September 1993**

Former England U21 international defender Jack Robinson began his career with Liverpool. He became the youngest player to represent the Anfield club when he made his debut aged just 16 years 250 days old. Valuable loan spells with Wolverhampton Wanderers and Blackpool preceeded a move to Queens Park Rangers in 2014. Robinson joined Forest in June 2018 and is approaching half-a-century of appearances in a Forest shirt.

Samba SOW

21

POSITION: Midfielder   **COUNTRY:** Mali   **DOB:** 29 April 1989

Defensive-midfielder Samba Sow was recruited from Dynamo Moscow on a two-year deal on the eve of the new 2019/20 Championship campaign. He made his Forest debut in the hard-fought 1-1 draw away to promotion favourites Leeds United when he replaced Tiago Silva in the second half at Elland Road. A full Mali international, with over 30 caps to his name, Sow's arrival brings additional competition for places in the Forest engine room.

THE 2019/20 SQUAD

Michael DAWSON

20

POSITION: Defender   **COUNTRY:** England   **DOB:** 18 November 1983

Now in his second spell at the City Ground, central-defender Michael Dawson returned to the club where his began his career, following successful spells with Tottenham Hotspur and Hull City. He rejoined Forest in 2018 and his huge experience has been of great benefit to the younger members of the Reds' squad. The former England international scored the first goal of his second stint with Forest during the 3-0 win over Birmingham City in August 2019.

Ryan YATES

22

POSITION: Midfielder   **COUNTRY:** England   **DOB:** 21 November 1997

Midfielder Ryan Yates has benefited from valuable loan spells with Barrow, Shrewsbury Town, Notts County and Scunthorpe United. In the summer of 2018, he agreed a new three-year deal at the City Ground and made his first-team debut against Bury in the League Cup. A first Forest goal came in the 2-2 draw away to West Bromwich Albion in February 2019 as Yates ended 2018/19 with 17 first-team appearances.

REWIND

The 2018/19 season saw a number of impressive Forest performances.

Here are three to remember...

ASTON VILLA 5
NOTTINGHAM FOREST 5

Easily the most entertaining game of the season took place at Villa Park in November as Forest and Aston Villa were involved in a ten-goal thriller.

Goals from Lewis Grabban, Joao Carvalho, Matty Cash and Joe Lolley had been cancelled out by four strikes from Villa striker Tammy Abraham, but Tobias Figueiredo's red card appeared to have turned the game in the home side's favour.

Anwar El Ghazi crashed in what seemed to be the winner with 15 minutes to go, but Grabban would go on to squeeze in a dramatic late equaliser to make sure the spoils were deservedly shared.

NOTTINGHAM FOREST 1
DERBY COUNTY 0

A frenetic and intriguing East Midlands derby ended in victory for Forest in February as Yohan Benalouane's early goal proved to be the difference between the two sides.

The defender reacted quickly from close range after Derby failed to deal with a Joe Lolley free-kick and the goal, inside 74 seconds, was enough to send the majority of the City Ground crowd home delighted.

Martyn Waghorn wasted a chance to equalise for the Rams when he went through on goal, but Forest kept themselves in control and saw the game out to earn a first East Midlands derby win since November 2015.

NOTTINGHAM FOREST 3
MIDDLESBROUGH 0

Arguably Nottingham Forest's best home performance of the season came in April as they comfortably beat Play-Off chasing Middlesbrough by three goals to nil at the City Ground.

Joe Lolley blasted home a first-half penalty after Karim Ansarifard had been fouled before Alexander Milosevic fired in his first goal for the club with a superb finish at the back post.

Forest were rampant and Joao Carvalho smashed a shot off the frame of the goal before he set up Lolley to slide the ball beyond Darren Randolph and put the seal on a thoroughly impressive win over Tony Pulis's side.

Answer these questions on the 2018/19 campaign and see how much attention you were paying LAST SEASON!

1. Who made the most league appearances for Forest last season?

ANSWER

2. Who netted Forest's first Championship goal last season?

ANSWER

3. How many points did Forest finish the 2018/19 season with?

ANSWER

4. How many Championship goals did Forest score last season?

ANSWER

5. What was the highest home attendance of 2018/19?

ANSWER

6. Against which club did Nottingham Forest hit four league goals?

ANSWER

7. Which club did Forest beat 10-9 on penalties in the EFL Cup first round?

ANSWER

8. Who knocked Forest out of the FA Cup in the third round?

ANSWER

9. Who received the most yellow cards in the league last season?

ANSWER

10. Which Forest player received a red card twice in the league during 2018/19?

ANSWER

11. Who did Forest sign from AIK during the January 2018 transfer window?

ANSWER

12. Who top-scored for Forest in the Championship last season?

ANSWER

ANSWERS ON PAGE 62

FAST FORWARD

There are lots of exciting games ahead for Forest in the second half of the 2019/20 Championship campaign.

Here are three potential crackers...

SATURDAY 8 FEBRUARY
LEEDS UNITED (H)

Leeds United are expected to be challenging at the top of the table once again this season and they visit the City Ground at the start of February.

Marcelo Bielsa's side missed out on promotion last time out and will provide another stern test for the Reds. It could be a crucial game in the promotion run-in and both sides will be looking to gain the maximum three points. If last season's game is anything to go by, with Forest coming out on top in a 4-2 thriller, it is sure to be a fiery afternoon on Trentside.

SATURDAY 4 APRIL
DERBY COUNTY (A)

The second East Midlands derby of the season takes place at the beginning of April with the bragging rights up for grabs once again.

The two sides will have already met once in November, following the clash at the City Ground, and the Reds will be hoping to head into the Easter weekend with a spring in their step and come away from their rivals with a first win at Pride Park since January 2015. Derby on the other hand will be hoping that Phillip Cocu can have a similar effect on the Rams to that of Frank Lampard last season in guiding them to the Play-Off final.

SATURDAY 2 MAY
STOKE CITY (H)

The curtain comes down on the 2019/20 Championship season with Stoke City the visitors to the City Ground in May.

The Reds will be hoping to have plenty to play for come the final day of the season, while the visitors will also have promotion aspirations of their own, so it could be a key fixture in deciding the final places at the top of the Championship. The two sides met on twice on Trentside last season, with Forest winning in the Carabao Cup, before the goalless stalemate in the league, and the Reds will be looking to end the season on a high against the Potters.

PREMIER LEAGUE

OUR PREDICTION FOR PREMIER LEAGUE WINNERS:

LIVERPOOL

YOUR PREDICTION:

OUR PREDICTION FOR PREMIER LEAGUE RUNNERS-UP:

MANCHESTER CITY

YOUR PREDICTION:

CHAMPIONSHIP

OUR PREDICTION FOR CHAMPIONSHIP WINNERS:

NOTTINGHAM FOREST

YOUR PREDICTION:

OUR PREDICTION FOR CHAMPIONSHIP RUNNERS-UP:

MIDDLESBROUGH

YOUR PREDICTION:

THE FA CUP

OUR PREDICTION FOR FA CUP WINNERS:

ARSENAL

YOUR PREDICTION:

OUR PREDICTION FOR FA CUP RUNNERS-UP:

TOTTENHAM HOTSPUR

YOUR PREDICTION:

EFL CUP

OUR PREDICTION FOR EFL CUP WINNERS:

SOUTHAMPTON

YOUR PREDICTION:

OUR PREDICTION FOR EFL CUP RUNNERS-UP:

LEICESTER CITY

YOUR PREDICTION:

2020 PREDICTIONS

FOREST

TEAM WORK

Every Championship team is hidden in the grid, except one!
Can you figure out which is missing?

Barnsley
Birmingham City
Blackburn Rovers
Brentford
Bristol City
Cardiff City
Charlton Athletic
Derby County
Fulham
Huddersfield Town
Hull City
Leeds United
Luton Town
Middlesbrough
Millwall
Nottingham Forest
Preston North End
Queens Park Rangers
Reading
Sheffield Wednesday
Stoke City
Swansea City
West Bromwich Albion
Wigan Athletic

```
A R D N E H T R O N N O T S E R P
D A O V Y U O B S C S A W U T V B
W Y T I C L O T S I R B F E V R N
A V U E R L E Q V P E Y I L C O U
I R M O W C Y U G D E N D A T L L
A P A B J I Z E J L U B H S L G U
T L H I C T X E S A T Y O A S Q T
Q C L G F Y E N V T S F W J K P O
P H U D D E R S F I E L D T O W N
I A F H M A S P V T L N R W X E T
W R D S B M I A O I F U C M Z S O
T L Y K H N E R M Y J Y A I R T W
A T S C A H S K G K L T R K T B N
P O A W R I V R J G N I D A E R R
H N I T A U C A K X U C I E V O L
N A O S O N H N W O L E F W H M P
J T S E B S S G T J C K F J G W N
P H M R N G B E V R V O C Q U I Y
C L V O E B G R A H G T I L O C T
A E B F K V P S E C A S T D R H I
Z T O M S G O E O N I B Y T B A C
V I F A E S F R B U T T E K S L M
O C W H O Q L B N R S F Y N E B A
F U C G B I T Q A R Y X O E L I H
O N H N R A M N W T U M I R D O G
U J A I Y T N U O C Y B R E D N N
N P D T L C V C P I D Z K P I B I
I E G T M S A O D J M F U C M P M
Y N K O X N D H A B O M A S A F R
E D T N O D E T I N U S D E E L I
W I G A N A T H L E T I C B T R B
```

34

ANSWERS ON PAGE 62

Q Ex-Hammer who made his debut for the Golden Boys last season

Middlesbrough keeper who played all 46 league games last season **R**

Joint Premier League top scorer last season alongside teammate Mané and Arsenal's Aubameyang

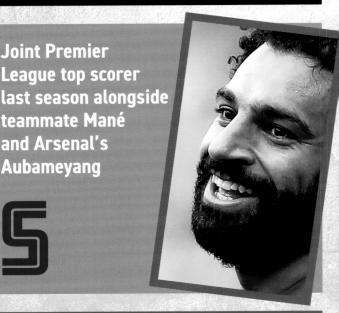

N France international who joined Spurs from Olympique Lyonnais in July 2019

S

O

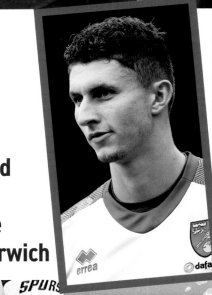

Goalkeeper and local lad who came through the ranks at Norwich

Nickname of Yorkshire club Barnsley **T**

U The Clarets' team kit manufacturer

Former England international in the manager's seat at Craven Cottage **P**

The home of Championship new boys Charlton Athletic **V**

W Managed the Blades to promotion to the Premier League

X Switzerland international who plays his home games at the Emirates Stadium

FOREST

A 2019/20 PART 2

WHO'S WHO & WHAT'S WHAT OF ENGLISH FOOTBALL?

Y Nottingham Forest's Argentine defensive midfielder

Z Hammers defender capped over 50 times by Argentina

ANSWERS ON PAGE 62

Joe
LOLLEY
23

POSITION: Midfielder   **COUNTRY:** England   **DOB:** 25 August 1992

A Premier League promotion-winner with Huddersfield Town, winger Joe Lolley joined Forest during the 2018 January transfer window. He enjoyed an impressive first full season at the City Ground in 2018/19, ending the campaign as the club's Player of the Season. Lolley began 2019/20 in fine form and was on target with goals against Birmingham City in the Championship and Derby County in the League Cup.

Claudio
YACOB
24

POSITION: Midfielder   **COUNTRY:** Argentina   **DOB:** 18 July 1987

Following six seasons in English football with West Bromwich Albion, Argentinian midfielder Claudio Yacob joined Forest in September 2018. He agreed a two-year deal at the City Ground and the defensive-minded midfielder made his Reds debut in a 1-0 home win over Sheffield United in November 2018. In total Yacob played in 16 Championship fixtures during his debut campaign with the club.

THE 2019/20 SQUAD

Tendayi DARIKWA — 27

POSITION: **Defender**   COUNTRY: **Zimbabwe**   DOB: **13 December 1991**

Nottingham-born defender Tendayi Darikwa has gained international recognition with Zimbabwe and joined his hometown club from Burnley in the summer of 2017. He began his career with Chesterfield before joining Burnley in 2015. He has made over 50 league appearances for Forest and will been keen to feature in Sabri Lamouchi plans for 2019/20.

Tiago SILVA — 28

POSITION: **Midfielder**   COUNTRY: **Portugal**   DOB: **2 June 1993**

Portuguese midfielder Tiago Silva put pen to paper on a two-year deal with Nottingham Forest in July 2019, having previously played all his football in his homeland with Belenenses and Feirense. Capped by Portugal at U21 and U23 level, Silva has gained the reputation as a goalscoring midfielder and netted his first goal in Forest colours in the 1-0 League Cup win over Fleetwood Town at the City Ground.

LEEDS UNITED
ELLAND ROAD
CAPACITY: 37,890

HUDDERSFIELD TOWN
THE JOHN SMITH'S STADIUM
CAPACITY: 24,500

BLACKBURN ROVERS
EWOOD PARK
CAPACITY: 31,367

PRESTON NORTH END
DEEPDALE
CAPACITY: 23,404

WIGAN ATHLETIC
DW STADIUM
CAPACITY: 25,133

BARNSLEY
OAKWELL
CAPACITY: 23,287

STOKE CITY
BET365 STADIUM
CAPACITY: 30,022

WEST BROMWICH ALBION
THE HAWTHORNS
CAPACITY: 26,850

BIRMINGHAM CITY
ST ANDREW'S
CAPACITY: 29,409

SWANSEA CITY
LIBERTY STADIUM
CAPACITY: 21,088

BRENTFORD
GRIFFIN PARK
CAPACITY: 12,763

CARDIFF CITY
CARDIFF CITY STADIUM
CAPACITY: 33,280

BRISTOL CITY
ASHTON GATE
CAPACITY: 27,000

READING
MADEJSKI STADIUM
CAPACITY: 24,161

MIDDLESBROUGH
RIVERSIDE STADIUM
CAPACITY: 34,742

HULL CITY
KCOM STADIUM
CAPACITY: 25,586

FOREST

CHAMPIONSHIP GROUNDS 2019/20

Take a look at where Forest will be heading this season to take on their rivals.

Tick the grounds off once we've visited!

SHEFFIELD WEDNESDAY
HILLSBOROUGH STADIUM
CAPACITY: 39,732

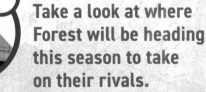

NOTTINGHAM FOREST
CITY GROUND
CAPACITY: 30,445

DERBY COUNTY
PRIDE PARK STADIUM
CAPACITY: 33,597

LUTON TOWN
KENILWORTH ROAD
CAPACITY: 10,356

QUEENS PARK RANGERS
KIYAN PRINCE FOUNDATION STADIUM
CAPACITY: 18,439

CHARLTON ATHLETIC
THE VALLEY
CAPACITY: 27,111

MILLWALL
THE DEN
CAPACITY: 20,146

FULHAM
CRAVEN COTTAGE
CAPACITY: 25,700

THE LEGEND
JOHN ROBERTSON

The arrival of Brian Clough at the City Ground proved the making of John Robertson. Clough instantly spotted Robertson's outstanding ability to run with the ball and cross with the most incredible accuracy. From the moment Clough walked into the City Ground, Robertson's career took off. His first taste of Forest success came in 1976/77 as Forest won promotion from the Second Division.

After helping win promotion to the top flight in 1976/77, Robertson gained further popularity with the Forest faithful when he netted the winning goal in the 1978 League Cup Final. After the Wembley final with Liverpool ended 0-0, Robertson converted from the penalty spot in the Old Trafford replay as Forest won the trophy for the first time in their history.

The League Cup win spurred Robertson and his teammates on to even greater achievements in 1977/78 as against all odds, they lifted the First Division title in their first season back in the top flight. Robertson ended the campaign as the side's ever-present top scorer with 12 league goals and a host of assists for strikers Peter Withe and Tony Woodcock.

Having landed the First Division title in 1978, Forest went on to even better things as they proceeded to lift the European Cup twelve months later. John Robertson was at the heart of this remarkable success as he crossed the ball for Trevor Francis to score the only goal of game in the final against Malmo.

Having been the creator of Forest's winning goal in the 1979 European Cup Final, John Robertson then added his name to scoresheet when the Reds retained their European title with a 1-0 win over Hamburg in 1980. Robertson squeezed his first-half shot past Hamburg 'keeper Rudolf Kargus as Forest once again lifted the greatest trophy in club football.

HEY REF!

Do you always know what the officials are signalling?

Take a look at these and see if you are up to the job...

1

2

3

4

44

5

8

6

9

7

10

Yohan BENALOUANE — 29

POSITION: **Defender**   COUNTRY: **Tunisia**   DOB: **28 March 1987**

Tunisian international defender Yohan Benalouane became former manager Martin O'Neill's first signing for Nottingham Forest when he joined the club in January 2019. Signed from Premier League Leicester City, Benalouane adds healthy competition to Forest's defensive line. He is blessed with both pace and power, alongside composure on the ball, which appear to make him an impressive option for Forest's 2019/20 Championship challenge.

THE 2019/20 SQUAD

Brice SAMBA — 30

POSITION: **Goalkeeper**   COUNTRY: **France**   DOB: **25 April 1994**

With the 2019/20 Championship season already underway, Forest increased their goalkeeping options with the signing of 25-year-old Brice Samba on 7 August 2019. The 'keeper joined Forest from French club Caen and made his debut for the Reds in the League Cup victory over Fleetwood. A Championship debut followed away to Fulham before Samba recorded his second clean sheet for the club in the 3-0 East Midlands derby success against Derby County in the League Cup.

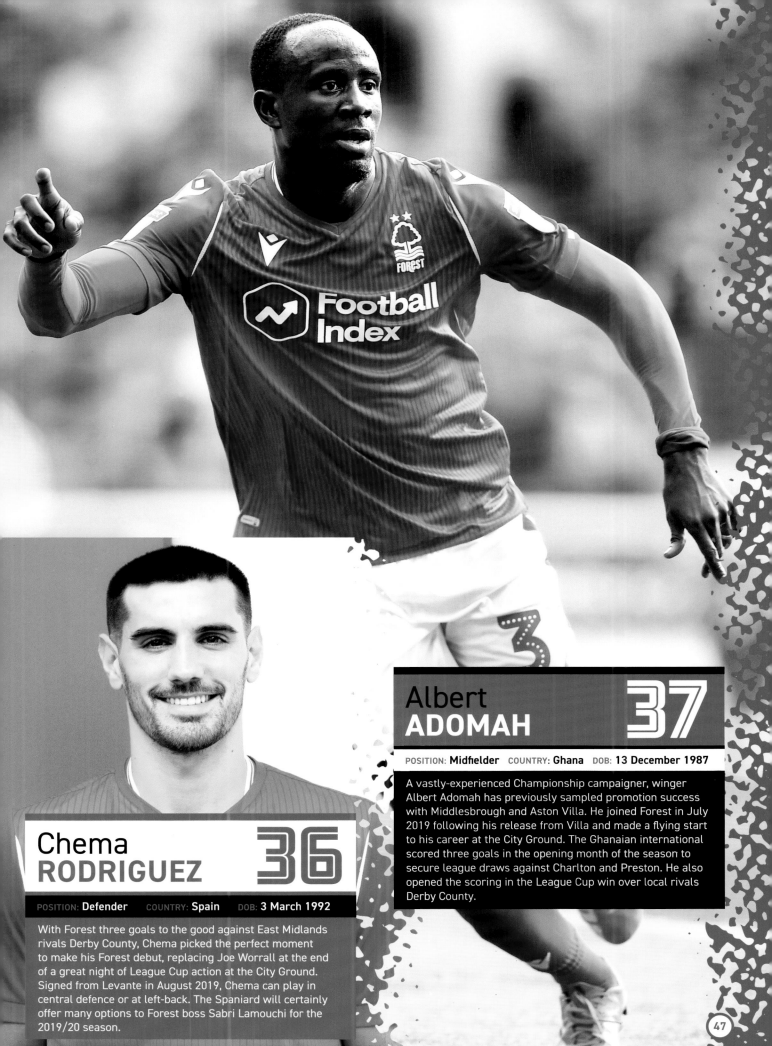

Albert ADOMAH 37

POSITION: **Midfielder**   COUNTRY: **Ghana**   DOB: **13 December 1987**

A vastly-experienced Championship campaigner, winger Albert Adomah has previously sampled promotion success with Middlesbrough and Aston Villa. He joined Forest in July 2019 following his release from Villa and made a flying start to his career at the City Ground. The Ghanaian international scored three goals in the opening month of the season to secure league draws against Charlton and Preston. He also opened the scoring in the League Cup win over local rivals Derby County.

Chema RODRIGUEZ 36

POSITION: **Defender**   COUNTRY: **Spain**   DOB: **3 March 1992**

With Forest three goals to the good against East Midlands rivals Derby County, Chema picked the perfect moment to make his Forest debut, replacing Joe Worrall at the end of a great night of League Cup action at the City Ground. Signed from Levante in August 2019, Chema can play in central defence or at left-back. The Spaniard will certainly offer many options to Forest boss Sabri Lamouchi for the 2019/20 season.

FOREST

THE LEGEND
STAN COLLYMORE

Having joined Nottingham Forest in the summer of 1993 for a £2M fee following a prolific spell with Southend United, Stan Collymore hammered home 19 First Division goals in 1993/94 during a memorable debut campaign at the City Ground. His impressive goals tally included the only goal of the game to sink neighbours Notts County 1-0 at the City Ground in October 1993.

Collymore's first season with Forest ended with promotion celebrations as Frank Clark's side returned to the Premier League at the first time of asking. Forest grabbed the runners-up spot behind champions Crystal Palace. Collymore's 19 goals played a big part in Forest's success and also presented the striker with the opportunity to play at the top level the following season.

If Collymore's first season at Forest was impressive, then his second was outstanding - the in-form striker hammered home 22 Premier League goals and 25 in all competitions. He began the season in fine form and never looked back. Collymore netted his first Premier League goal in Forest's opening home game of the season - a 1-1 draw with Premier League champions Manchester United.

Collymore's 22-goal haul proved the catalyst for an outstanding season as the club marked their return to the top flight with a third-placed finish. Among the goals, Collymore netted a brace in the Reds' most comprehensive win of the season as they made fools of Sheffield Wednesday with a 7-1 win at Hillsborough on 1 April 1995.

After such a successful season at club level, Collymore was rewarded with an England call-up for the Umbro Cup in the summer of 1995. Stan made his England debut while still a Forest player when he partnered Alan Shearer in a 2-1 victory over Japan at Wembley on 3 June 1995.

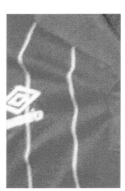

THE CHAMPIONSHIP

BARNSLEY

BIRMINGHAM CITY

BLACKBURN ROVERS

BRENTFORD

BRISTOL CITY

CARDIFF CITY

CHARLTON ATHLETIC

DERBY COUNTY

FULHAM

HUDDERSFIELD TOWN

HULL CITY

LEEDS UNITED

2019/20

In Forest's red and white world, get to know your rivals in full Championship colour!

LUTON TOWN

MIDDLESBROUGH

MILLWALL

NOTTINGHAM FOREST

PRESTON NORTH END

QUEENS PARK RANGERS

READING

SHEFFIELD WEDNESDAY

STOKE CITY

SWANSEA CITY

WEST BROMWICH ALBION

WIGAN ATHLETIC

51

FOREST

JOE LOLLEY

2018/19

PLAYER OF THE SEASON

Following a sublime season, Joe Lolley was voted as the Nottingham Forest Player of the Year for the 2018/19 season.

The winger was an ever-present for the Reds, featuring in all 46 league games and all cup games as he performed impressively throughout.

He said: "I'm delighted; it means a lot. The fans have voted for me and I would like to say thank you to everyone who voted.

"Individually, I had a good season. It would have been nice, as a team, to have got to the Play-Offs, but it didn't work out. But from an individual point of view it was a good season and to be recognised for that is a good feeling.

"It was probably my first full season in football without injuries. I haven't had the longest career in football, but it was my first season fully-fit and it gives me a platform to kick on from."

With 12 goals and 11 assists to his name last season, Lolley was at the forefront of Forest's attacking play and following thousands of fans' votes, he was crowned the winner.

Lolley picked up 56 per cent of the vote, with Jack Colback in second and Joao Carvalho in third.

A standout game of last season for Lolley came at Villa Park, as he contributed four assists and scored once in the thrilling 5-5 draw against Aston Villa.

He also scored fine strikes against Birmingham at home and Middlesbrough away, as well as finding the net in away victories at Hull and Bolton.

Brennan JOHNSON 40

POSITION: **Striker**   COUNTRY: **England**   DOB: **23 May 2001**

The local boy making good, Nottingham-born Brennan Johnson joined the Forest Academy as an eight-year-old and has progressed through the age groups to play first-team football at the City Ground. The forward got his first-team opportunity on the opening day of the 2019/20 season when he replaced Alfa Semedo in the closing stages against West Bromwich Albion. Johnson is a young man with a bright future and one to watch over the coming months.

Zach CLOUGH 39

POSITION: **Striker**   COUNTRY: **England**   DOB: **8 March 1995**

Forward Zach Clough arrived at the City Ground during the 2017 January transfer window. A star performer at Championship level, Clough's move to Forest offered the clever frontman a route back to the Championship following Bolton's drop to League One. With the ability to operate in a number of attacking roles, Clough will be keen to make his mark with Forest in 2019/20 after spending last season on loan at Rochdale.

Michael HEFELE 44

POSITION: Defender **COUNTRY:** Germany **DOB:** 1 September 1990

Defender Michael Hefele joined Forest in the summer of 2018 from Huddersfield Town. A key player in the Terriers' 2016/17 promotion success, Hefele found first-team chances hard to come by with Huddersfield at Premier League level and jumped at the chance of a switch to the City Ground. The German defender featured in 18 matches in his debut season with the Reds.

THE 2019/20 SQUAD

Aro MURIC 49

POSITION: Goalkeeper **COUNTRY:** Kosovo **DOB:** 7 November 1998

Kosovan international goalkeeper Arijanet Muric joined Forest in July 2019 on a season-long loan from Premier League champions Manchester City. Standing 6ft 6ins, Muric is a commanding figure who is highly rated by his parent club. He made his Forest debut on the opening day of the season and kept his first clean sheet for Forest as the Reds registered a 3-0 home win over Birmingham City.

The City Ground

Nottingham   NG2

COVER THE WALL IN POSTERS!

FOREST

Forest have boasted a wealth of talent over the years! Here is our...

FOREST DREAM TEAM

...see if you agree!

GOALKEEPER

SHILTON
1

PETER SHILTON

Legendary England goalkeeper Peter Shilton played over 200 league games for Forest between 1977 and 1982. He enjoyed a trophy-laden career at the City Ground as Forest secured both domestic and European success.

YOUR CHOICE

DEFENDER

ANDERSON
2

VIV ANDERSON

Nottingham-born Viv Anderson enjoyed phenomenal success with his local club as Forest enjoyed their greatest period of success in the late '70s and early '80s. A member of the club's 1977/78 First Division title-winning team, he won the first of his 30 England caps while at the City Ground.

YOUR CHOICE

MIDFIELDER

O'NEILL
6

MARTIN O'NEILL

A key performer in the golden era at the City Ground, midfielder Martin O'Neill's career blossomed under the management of Brian Clough. A Second Division promotion-winner and First Division champion, injury saw O'Neill on the bench for Forest's first European Cup success before playing in the second final as Forest overcame Hamburg 1-0 in 1980.

YOUR CHOICE

MIDFIELDER

KEANE
7

ROY KEANE

All-action midfielder Roy Keane proved to be a shrewd signing by Nottingham Forest in the summer of 1990 after joining from Irish club Cobh Ramblers for £47,000. Keane was a star performer in the Forest team that reached the 1991 FA Cup Final and then tasted Wembley glory in the Full Members Cup in 1991/92.

YOUR CHOICE

MIDFIELDER

GEMMILL
8

ARCHIE GEMMILL

Scotland international Archie Gemmill was one of many players that played for Brian Clough at Derby County before moving on to join their former boss at the City Ground. Signed for a fee of £25,000 - Gemmill was a First Division title-winner and two-time European champion with Forest.

YOUR CHOICE

DEFENDER

PEARCE 3

STUART PEARCE

A true cult-hero with the City Ground faithful, Stuart Pearce played 524 games for the club over a 12-year period. An inspirational captain, Pearce led Forest to back-to-back League Cup Final victories and was named the club's Player of the Season on three occasions.

YOUR CHOICE

DEFENDER

BURNS 4

KENNY BURNS

Recruited from Birmingham City, the powerful and committed performances of central-defender Kenny Burns proved vital as Forest were crowned First Division champions in 1978. The Scottish international also played a vital role in both of the club's European Cup successes in 1979 and 1980.

YOUR CHOICE

DEFENDER

WALKER 5

DES WALKER

Blessed with electric pace, central defender Des Walker was a double League Cup-winner with Forest in 1989 and 1990. After spells with Sampdoria and Sheffield Wednesday, Walker returned to Forest in 2002/03 and over his two spells at the City Ground he played over 400 games for the club.

YOUR CHOICE

FORWARD

STOREY-MOORE 9

IAN STOREY-MOORE

Goalscoring wideman Ian Storey-Moore netted a highly-impressive 105 league goals for Forest in 236 league outings while at the City Ground. His Forest career spanned between 1962 and 1972. He won England recognition while at Forest and later played for Manchester United.

YOUR CHOICE

FORWARD

FRANCIS 10

TREVOR FRANCIS

Trevor Francis was the scorer of the famous goal that secured Nottingham Forest the first of their two European Cup titles. Francis met a John Robertson cross on the stroke of half-time to net the game's only goal against Malmo in 1979.

YOUR CHOICE

FORWARD

ROBERTSON 11

JOHN ROBERTSON

Viewed by many as Nottingham Forest's greatest player, John Robertson was blessed with great close control and outstanding ability to cross a ball with pin-point accuracy. He scored the only goal of the game to secure Forest's second European Cup success as they defeated Hamburg 1-0 in 1980.

YOUR CHOICE

TOP 10

MY TOP 10...

MOMENTS OF THIS YEAR

1.
2.
3.
4.
5.
6.
7.
8.
9.
10.

MY TOP 10...

FOOTBALLERS OF ALL TIME

1.
2.
3.
4.
5.
6.
7.
8.
9.
10.

MY TOP 10...

FOREST MEMORIES

1.
2.
3.
4.
5.
6.
7.
8.
9.
10.

MY TOP 10...

RESOLUTIONS FOR 2020

1.
2.
3.
4.
5.
6.
7.
8.
9.
10.

QUIZ ANSWERS

PAGE 14 · A-Z PART ONE

A. César Azpilicueta. B. Bristol City.
C. Matty Cash. D. Harlee Dean. E. The Eagles.
F. Thomas Frank, Brentford. G. Goodison Park.
H. Neil Harris. I. Kelechi Iheanacho.
J. Gabriel Jesus. K. Mateusz Klich.
L. Jesse Lingard. M. Glenn Murray.

PAGE 20 · FAN'TASTIC

Owen Farrell, Lewis Hamilton Johanna Konta,
Anthony Joshua and Ben Stokes.

PAGE 24 · FACE OFF!

A. Matty Cash. B. Michael Dawson.
C. Jack Robinson. D. Albert Adomah.
E. Alexander Milosevic

1. Ben Watson. 2. Joe Worrall. 3. Alfa Semedo.
4. Joe Lolley. 5. Costel Pantilimon.
6. Tendayi Darikwa. 7. Sammy Ameobi.
8. Yuri Ribeiro. 9. Lewis Grabban

PAGE 31 · REWIND

1. Joe Lolley, 46. 2. Daryl Murphy v Bristol City.
3. 66. 4. 61. 5. 29,530 v Leeds United.
6. Leeds United. 7. Bury. 8. Chelsea.
9. Jack Colback, 15. 10. Yohan Benalouane.
11. Alexander Milošević. 12. Lewis Grabban, 16.

PAGE 34 · TEAM WORK

Sheffield Wednesday.

PAGE 36 · A-Z PART TWO

N. Tanguy Ndombele. O. Aston Oxborough.
P. Scott Parker. Q. Domingos Quina
R. Darren Randolph. S. Mo Salah. T. The Tykes.
U. Umbro. V. The Valley. W. Chris Wilder.
X. Granit Xhaka. Y. Claudio Yacob.
Z. Pablo Zabaleta.

PAGE 44 · HEY REF

1. Direct free kick. 2. Indirect free kick.
3. Yellow card - Caution. 4. Red card - Sending off.
5. Obstruction. 6. Substitution. 7. Offside/foul.
8. Penalty. 9. Offside location. 10. Play on.

THIS BOOK BELONGS TO...

FOREST

Name:

Age:

Favourite player:

2019/2020

My Predictions...	Actual...
Forest's final position:	
Forest's top scorer:	
Championship winners:	
Championship top scorer:	
FA Cup winners:	
EFL Cup winners:	

Contributors: Peter Rogers

A TWOCAN PUBLICATION

©2019. Published by twocan under licence from Nottingham Forest FC.

Every effort has been made to ensure the accuracy of information within this publication but the publishers cannot be held responsible for any errors or omissions. Views expressed are those of the authors and do not necessarily represent those of the publishers or the football club. All rights reserved.

ISBN: 978-1-911502-77-7

PICTURE CREDITS: Action Images, Press Association, Rex by Shutterstock.

£9